Explore the secret routes of the skies
from a bird's-eye view . . .

MYA-ROSE CRAIG

Illustrated by Lynn Scurfield

PUFFIN

CONTENTS

INTRODUCTION

Look around you. Whether you're standing in a field or a town park, if you wait a few minutes, the chances are that you will see a bird. It may be high above your head, or on the ground searching for juicy worms to eat.

I used to notice the birds changing with the seasons and wonder where they went. Here's their secret . . . many of these creatures go on epic journeys every single year. I've been fortunate enough to travel the world and come across the remarkable journeys of those birds, and I want to tell you their stories.

I'm still astonished by the adventures they have. The Arctic Tern, which is small enough to fit in the palm of my hand, can fly around the world, from pole to pole, every single year. Millions of birds fly incredible distances across continents, over mountains and even oceans. They travel on bird highways – routes in the sky – that are followed by each new generation.

These journeys are called migration, and it's tough. Imagine waking up in the morning and walking as far as you can, grabbing a bite to eat (if you are lucky), before finding a safe place to sleep, and then doing this the next day . . . and the next . . . and the next, until you finally arrive at your new home.

So why do birds do it? They're searching for a place that's easier for them to live, with enough food, a place they can raise their young. They may also follow the seasons, escaping from weather that is too hot or too cold for them.

Most migrating birds head north in the northern spring and south in the autumn, to make the most of the long, warm summer days, which are perfect for nesting. Birds seem to know when it is time to migrate, becoming restless. They probably pick up clues from the changes in day length, changing temperatures and food supplies, and they inherit these instincts from their parents.

Some of these migration routes cover thousands of miles, so how do birds know where to go? Scientists are still trying to figure some of this out, but they do know that birds can find their way using the position of the sun in the day and the stars at night. They also look for landmarks, such as the mountains and rivers that they fly over. Some can even sense magnetic fields – which is like having a mini compass in their heads.

Next time you spot a bird close to where you live, just think, a few weeks ago it may have been living on the other side of the world! So, it's time to explore the exciting journeys of seven different birds. I hope this book helps you to fly high as we take to the skies . . .

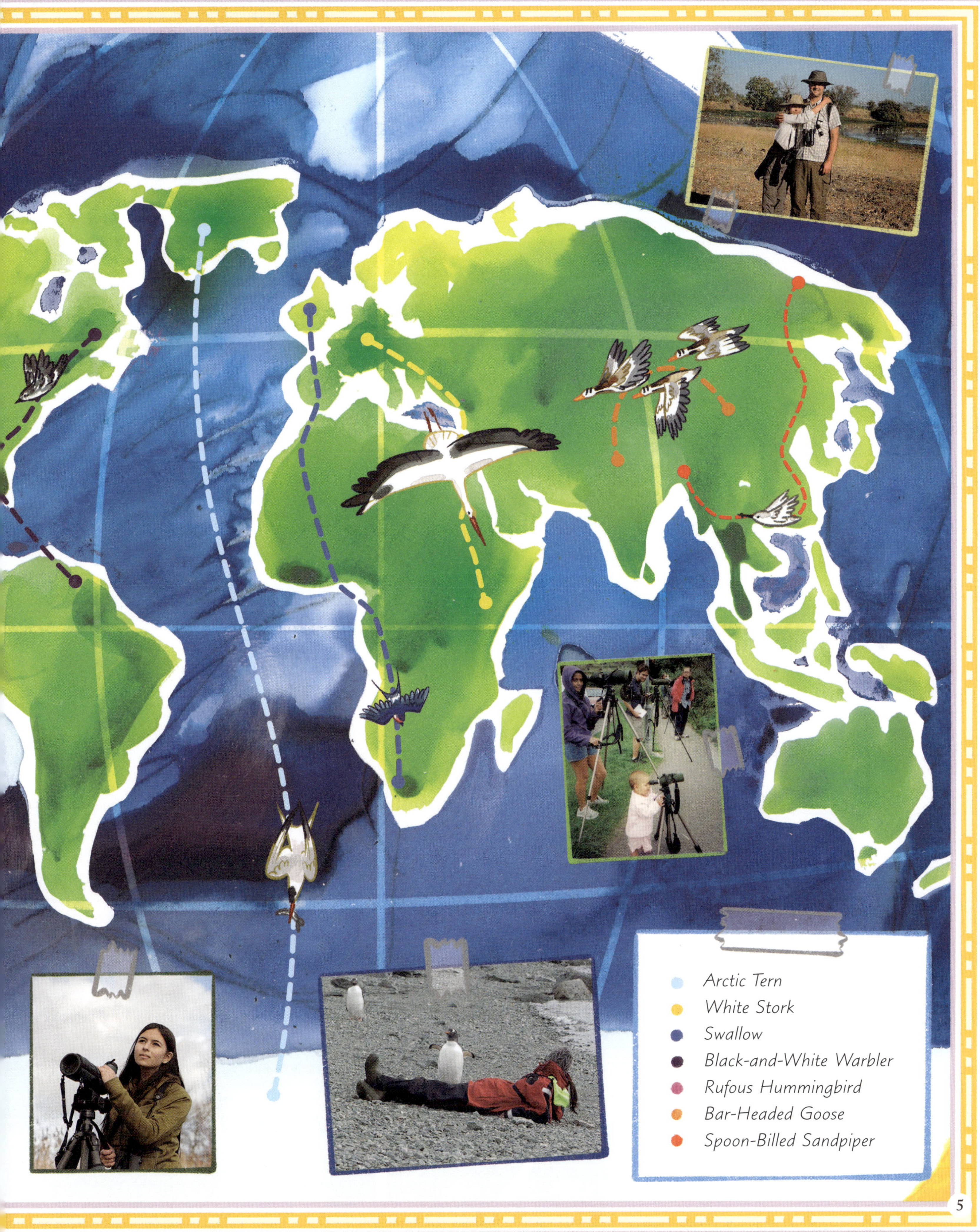
Arctic Tern
White Stork
Swallow
Black-and-White Warbler
Rufous Hummingbird
Bar-Headed Goose
Spoon-Billed Sandpiper

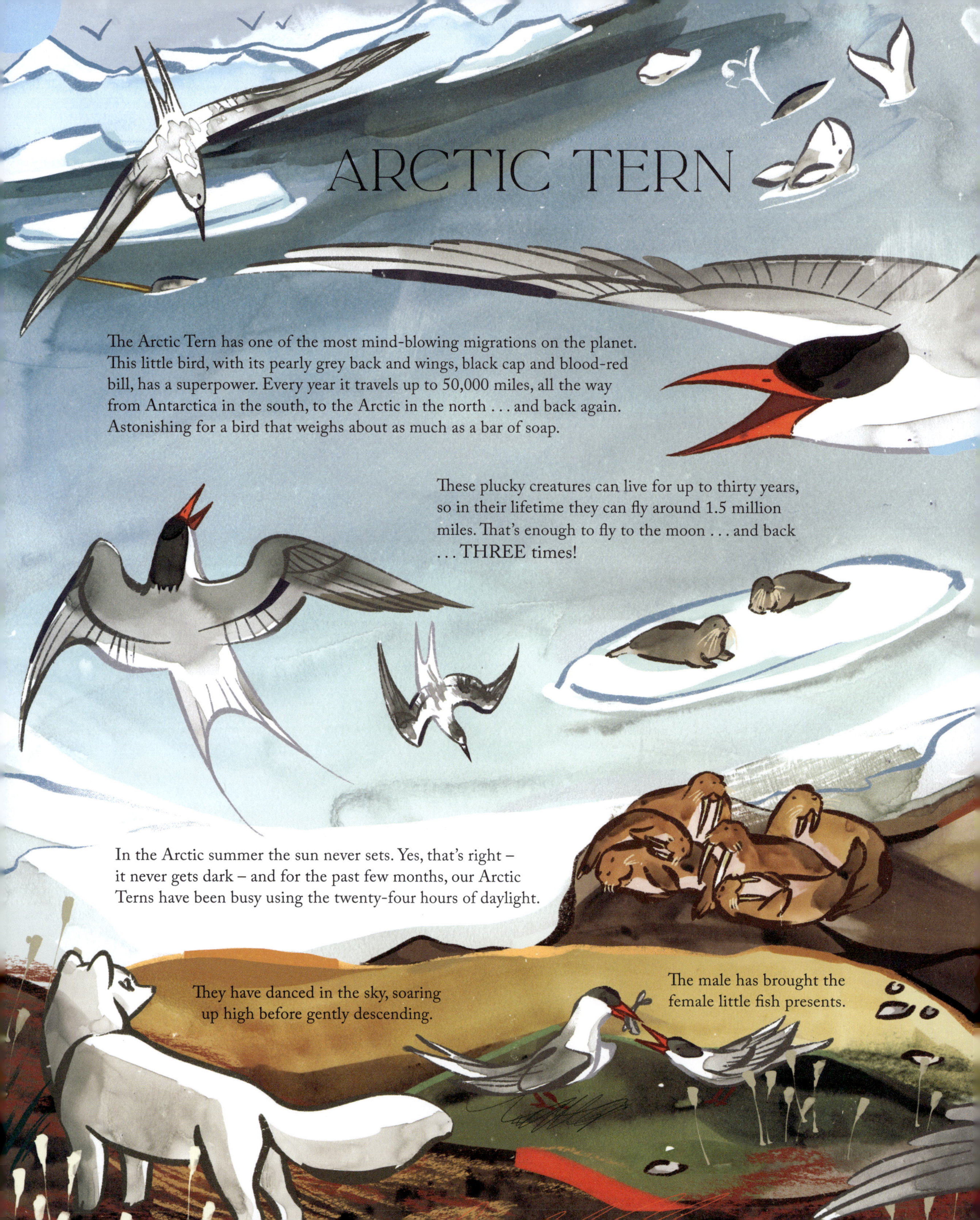

ARCTIC TERN

The Arctic Tern has one of the most mind-blowing migrations on the planet. This little bird, with its pearly grey back and wings, black cap and blood-red bill, has a superpower. Every year it travels up to 50,000 miles, all the way from Antarctica in the south, to the Arctic in the north . . . and back again. Astonishing for a bird that weighs about as much as a bar of soap.

These plucky creatures can live for up to thirty years, so in their lifetime they can fly around 1.5 million miles. That's enough to fly to the moon . . . and back . . . THREE times!

In the Arctic summer the sun never sets. Yes, that's right – it never gets dark – and for the past few months, our Arctic Terns have been busy using the twenty-four hours of daylight.

They have danced in the sky, soaring up high before gently descending.

The male has brought the female little fish presents.

Then, when they were both ready, they built their simple little nest on the ground among the nests of their friends. Once their two eggs hatched, they spent all their time flying back and forth . . .

back and forth . . .

catching fish to feed their chicks.

They barely had time to feed themselves, and then it was time to head south again. Winter was coming, the wind was getting stronger and a sprinkling of snow was beginning to dust the tundra. Even the sun began to set at night for a couple of hours. The parents won't see each other until next summer, when they're back in the Arctic. Until then they'll brave the long journey alone.

It's time to begin. Our Arctic Tern lifts off excitedly, eager to start her journey. Her long, thin wings and tail streamers are perfectly shaped for cutting through the air and catching the wind. Hollow bones, like the frame of a kite, make her even lighter.

Our tern knows she is made to fly.

As the flock takes off and heads out over the sea, she quickly joins them. Watching them through my binoculars, I feel their freedom as they take to the air. The birdwatchers wave – we know the seasons are changing now the Arctic Terns are leaving . . .

WHITE STORK

For many years our White Stork has returned every spring to the same barn roof in the middle of Germany, where she and her mate once carefully constructed a huge nest of sticks on top of the chimney there.

Each year they add a little bit more, and now the nest is taller than they are. It is so large that house sparrows and starlings build their own nests inside it! It's been a good year, with lots of food in the nearby meadows, and beetles, grasshoppers and frogs in the damper areas. They have watched their chicks grow from balls of fluff to their full enormous size. The chicks test their huge black-and-white wings by standing on top of their nest and frantically flapping.

In the olden days, people used to tell stories about storks carrying babies with them in a cloth bundle when they returned in the spring. They'd drop them down the chimney to the hopeful family. Children would sing to the storks or put sweets for them on the windowsill.

Two sisters who watched the storks from their house thought this was a funny idea. Everyone knows where babies really come from! They were fascinated by the storks, though. Every day before school, they would look for the chicks in their big nest on top of the barn. Sometimes – if they were lucky – they would spot a young bird peering right back at them. By the end of the summer, the young birds had grown as big as their parents and the girls knew that it was nearly time for them to go.

Other storks start passing overhead, their long necks stretching towards the south. Our White Stork gazes up from her nest and she takes one, two, three flaps of her mighty wings. She soars upwards to join them.

They'll be back next spring. Our same white stork will join her partner, raising another fluffy brood. But first, she's going on her travels . . .

More and more storks fly up from their nesting places to join the flock as it passes overhead. Very soon there are thousands of birds gathered in the sky, all heading in the same direction.

Storks have enormous wings, measuring two metres across – that's almost as tall as you on a friend's shoulders! Their wings are very big and heavy, and flapping takes a lot of effort. So once storks are up in the air, they stretch out their wings and catch the warm air swirling below them.

These thermals lift them higher and higher, carrying them over long distances as they glide on their outstretched wings.

The warm thermals rise from the land but not the sea, so storks don't like to fly for too long over water. Our stork and the flock head south and then east, avoiding the water by crossing a thin piece of land, called an isthmus, and arriving in Turkey. The rectangular tiled roofs where they built their nest are replaced with the domed ceilings of the city ahead.

Their journey isn't over, as they swoop around the Mediterranean Sea and then glide over Egypt. They fly over the mouth of the enormous River Nile. Beneath them is harsh golden desert, but along the Nile, the longest river in the world, everything is luscious green and shimmering blue.

Our stork is hungry now. The edges of the river are the perfect hunting grounds, so, balanced on her long legs, she wades through the shallow water without getting soggy feathers.
She is the best at playing statues – she can wait for hours without moving,
and then . . .
there!
A frog, fish or another tasty snack. Before it spots her, her massive red bill darts down and snatches it out of the water. She swallows the snack in one big gulp.
GULP!

But she can't stay in Egypt – she must fly onwards to her winter home in Kenya. Other storks are already scattered across the savannah, hundreds of them, all of them clattering their bills in greeting to one another. Storks can't sing like most birds, and so instead they hiss and screech at each other. It sounds just like they are delighted to see old friends.

She spies a lagoon, which looks promising – travelling across continents is hungry work. Unlike in her summer home, she isn't the biggest animal by the water and she has to be careful she doesn't become something else's snack. Lions, zebras and antelope are drinking on the banks, hippos are lounging about in the mud, soaking up the sun, while crocodiles are lying in wait. She plucks a toad from the edge of the water and gobbles it down, startling a cloud of smaller birds who were hiding in the reeds.

The lagoon is full of life.

If you lived here you might notice the white birds scattered across the landscape. The storks have returned! It's exciting to think of the amazing journeys that so many birds make every single year . . .

SWALLOW

A very long time ago, before even your parents were born, people wondered where Barn Swallows disappeared to every autumn and reappeared from every spring. As soon as the autumn leaves appeared, the birds would gather in large flocks in the evening, but the next morning they would be gone. Some people even thought they must have flown to the Moon, but others agreed this couldn't be right.

Eager to know what was happening to the Barn Swallows, the people followed them to the reedbeds where they went to sleep. The roosting swallows would land on the reeds in their thousands, twittering and calling 'goodnight, sleep well' to each other.

The very next day, not a single bird was left.

After seeing the swallows disappear into the reeds overnight, the people figured they must be burying themselves in the mud beneath them. Tucking themselves away before winter like a bear in a cave. Of course! After all, where else could the birds be going?

Nowadays, we know that swallows are doing something much more impressive: they fly over 6,000 miles – all the way to South Africa. We're going to lift off and see what they're really up to on their journey . . .

Our swallows have spent the long summer days building their cup-shaped mud-and-grass nest under the eaves of a house. Here they laid their eggs and fed their young on insects until, in September, the whole family was ready to head south. They must leave before the days become shorter, the nights become longer and colder, and their feast of flies disappears for the winter.

Watch them as they join the huge, chattering, swirling flocks that gather on the telephone wires strung between poles and houses.

I smile when I see my first swallow of the year, because I know then that the summer is coming. But now the seasons are changing again – our swallows are restless – they are eager to begin their long journey south.

A huge swarming mass of arrow-shaped bodies, twisting and turning effortlessly through the air as they gulp down insects.

The flocks get bigger and bigger as they are joined by swallows from other parts of the UK and the rest of Europe.

You gaze up in amazement as the birds stream above you, heading through France and then onwards.

The parents from our nest will take different routes: the mother heads to Spain and Gibraltar, and the father travels through Italy and Sicily, before funnelling over the Mediterranean Sea at its narrowest points. They must avoid long stretches of open water so they can find a safe reedbed for their night-time rest.

Now they head into northern Africa and as they fly, they must watch out for Eleonora's falcons, which will swoop off their cliff-ledge nest, looking to carry a tasty morsel back to feed their own chicks.

Onwards they fly, through Morocco and Tunisia, snatching insects as they go, and skimming ponds with their open bills to drink water as they fly. They don't have time to stop. They are about to arrive at the single biggest obstacle of their journey: the Sahara Desert.

Over a thousand miles of rolling sand, with nothing to eat or drink. The scorching sun beats down relentlessly during the day and the nights are shiveringly cold. The clear skies ahead are suddenly blotted out by a sandstorm whipped up by the whistling winds.

All around her, the mother bird can see dozens of other swallows braving the same journey. Some of them are the birds that gathered on the wires with her in England, others she has met on the way through Europe.

For some of them the challenge of the desert will be too much, and they will die and fall into the sand.

She flies . . .

and flies . . .

and flies . . .

She wonders if her partner is somewhere nearby, making the same journey.

She must go all the way down to the bottom of Africa in just a few weeks.

The children wave to her as she passes Elmina Castle on the coast of Ghana, and she knows she is halfway to her final destination. She spies lions and elephants, hippos and crocodiles, giraffes and zebras, and all kinds of exotic birds as she heads onwards.

She flies and flies and flies.

Finally, after six weeks, she arrives at the tip of South Africa. Our swallow is exhausted! She wants a PROPER rest – it has been a long and tiring journey, but she is glad to be somewhere warm and safe, with plenty to eat again. She spends her last few soaring moments in the air, before she lands on the twig of a dead branch beside a large pond in the middle of Cape Town, victorious.

Another migration completed!

All around her she can see other swallows too, equally tired out from their long flights.

Then, suddenly – there! She spies her partner, already comfortably settled into the South African lifestyle, skillfully hawking insects over the water. She joins him, delighted. 'Hello, hello,' they chatter to each other. This will be their new home for the next five months.

Behind them, the kids of the city have crept out into the park – some with binoculars – to spy their first look at the new arrivals. They grin and smile at one other. A cheer goes up – their swallows have returned home once again. It is springtime in South Africa!

ARCTIC TERN

All this time, while we've been travelling with other birds, our Arctic Tern has been flying and flying. We see her now, in a white cloud of terns that rolls over the Atlantic Ocean.

Far out to sea they zig-zag their way south, using the wind to help them on their way, dodging the worst of the storms.

The sharp vision of our tern catches a movement below the surface of the sea. She dives without warning, dropping through the sky, folds her wings into her body, pierces the water and . . .

. . . snaps up a fish in her bill. All this flying is making her peckish!

At night, the terns don't have time to stop,
so they sleep as they glide over the sea.
They still have a long way to go . . .

BLACK-AND-WHITE WARBLER

Deep in a dark, damp forest in eastern Canada, at the base of a large tree, tucked away from sight among the rocks and roots, lies the nest of our Black-and-White Warbler.

In the spring she had spent weeks carefully crafting it from twigs and moss before laying her five creamy-white eggs. Now, three months later, her chicks are fully grown and have left the nest, and she is fat and full of food.

Her job here is done and even though it is still the height of summer, she gets a feeling deep in her bones. A feeling that it is time to leave. She prefers to migrate at night, and there is nothing stopping her as she waits for darkness to fall, before launching herself off a branch and starting her journey south.

Black-and-White Warblers don't need to wait for the weather to get colder or the days to get shorter before they start preparing to leave for the winter. No, instead they are often the first to fly. The start of their migration is the sign to the other birds that it's time to pack up and move on.

Our warbler enters the urban jungle of New York, USA. She is surrounded by tall buildings pushing up towards the clouds, their glass walls an invisible obstacle for her to avoid. She keeps an eye out for their glinting reflection as honking yellow taxis shuffle slowly through the queues of traffic beneath her.

Flocks of pigeons watch warily for a passing peregrine that may pluck them from the sky for dinner. But then, there, in the middle of all this busy chaos – a patch of green!

If you were in Central Park, you might see our warbler looking down at you. The park is lush with trees and filled with other migrating warblers, all looking for a place to rest.

There is a lake with geese and ducks and a great egret fishing in one corner. The tree on its banks looks like a good spot. Our warbler may be small, but she is ready to defend her patch of mossy heaven, as she chases away a pair of red-breasted nuthatches.

The birdwatchers stand on the bridge, searching for her . . . there! She grips on to the bark with her long, strong claws and walks down the side of the trunk looking for food. Soon enough she finds some insects: jackpot! Finally full, she sits on a branch and ruffles her feathers, happy.

It's time to fly again, and our Black-and-White Warbler hugs the coast, keeping the ocean to the east. Next stop is Cape May, where she makes an appearance to entertain the birdwatchers at the bird observatory.

As she heads on with her journey, she rests and feeds in whatever patches of woodland she can find. These patches become smaller each year.

She presses on, reaching Florida and the Everglades National Park. Suddenly there is water as far as the eye can see, but she can't stop yet. Launching herself out over the waves, the wind buffeting her, she flies towards Cuba.

Around her are other tiny birds flying out to sea. Most of them, like her, only venture out over the water during their migration. They are more at home hopping around in trees than making oceanic voyages.

After her flight over the ocean, she arrives in a forest, dense and dark, with a thick mist hanging over it like a blanket. It is damp and humid, bursting with life and plenty of food. Our warbler flutters down onto a branch, soggy and tired.

Other small birds are arriving too – thousands will arrive in the coming weeks. Out of the corner of her eye, she sees another Black-and-White Warbler! She chirps out a greeting, welcoming him to the island, but when he responds she notices his different accent. He spends his summers much further south than her in a marshy wood on the east coast of the USA, and plans to stay in Cuba for the winter, just like his parents before him.

But she has other plans.

Our warbler starts to fly over the Cuban mountains and through the forest, eventually so high that the clouds are below her.

There is one more leg of the journey she will make before she stops flying. Once again, our Black-and-White Warbler

flies out to sea . . .

. . . and, finally, she reaches Venezuela. On the slopes of her new hillside home there is a thick forest, where the resident birds constantly call to each other. Below are tightly packed houses, tumbling down the slope with trees squeezed amongst them. Our warbler flits between the two.

Some days she stays in the woodland, picking apart tree bark to find her next meal. She scurries up and down the trees, earning her nickname of 'creeper', uncovering feast after feast of insects tucked in the bark.

Snakes wind their way through the maze of branches, the occasional monkey leaps across the canopy, and sloths laze away the days. There could be nowhere better to spend the winter, thinks our warbler.

Below her are the humans and the houses, and on other days she will forage for food amongst the branches there. The children of the street notice the stripy little warbler hanging around in their trees. They peer out of their windows each morning to watch for their new friend.

After a while she knows she must head north again. She's always leaving, always returning, on her long journey.

RUFOUS HUMMINGBIRD

This summer has been a busy time for our Rufous Hummingbird. First, she had to pick out a male bird to raise her chicks with – always a tricky choice. For days, male birds swirled in circles around her – climbing higher and higher until they dived down towards the ground, buzzing as the wind whistled through their wing and tail feathers.

Perched out on a branch, she watched them closely to judge their dancing skills.

The first was a little too slow, she thought,

the second a little too fast and out of control.

But the third was talented enough to deserve her attention.

Her breeding partner's throat shone an iridescent red and his body was the colour of copper coins.

Their three chicks demanded constant food, and from dawn until dusk, their parents drank the nectar of flowers and caught hundreds of insects to feed their babies. They regurgitated these delicious meals into their chicks' open bills. Now, finally, the young birds are fully grown.

Compared to the length of their body, Rufous Hummingbirds have the longest migration of any bird in the world. Our bird has spent her summer in Alaska, the green tundra full of flowers and insects, but soon snow will cover the landscape and she knows she must be long gone by then.

So she will head south, making a 3,000-mile journey down to the hot sun of western Mexico.

But how is she going to travel all that way?

A long time ago, people didn't think it was possible. Hummingbirds are such small birds, some of them tiny enough to be mistaken for insects, and their wings are so short that they don't seem designed for long-distance flying – only for hovering by flowers to feed. So how were they travelling such a long way?

There is a bird who is well-known for migrating long distances, which is big and strong enough to make these journeys – a goose. So it was obvious really – hummingbirds must be hitching a ride on the backs of geese so they could travel between their summer and winter homes. The mystery of how hummingbirds migrated had finally been solved: there was a goose taxi service!

In reality, several species of hummingbirds migrate, and they are totally able to fly by themselves – no geese needed! So, having stuffed herself full of flower nectar, which her body has converted to fat to use as fuel during her long journey, our hummingbird sets off.

She has an amazing memory. She knows exactly where she is migrating to and from each year, where she will live all winter, and where she is going to lay her eggs in the summer.

That's not all: she even remembers the places on her journey that grow patches of flowers, perfect for her to refuel.

Arriving in California, she visits one of her favourite spots – one she has stopped at every year since she hatched. It is in the middle of the city, surrounded by roaring streets and busy pavements.

Inside the fence, it is bright with colour and from every branch there are hummingbird feeders hanging – plastic tubes filled with sugary water that tastes as good as anything she could sip from an actual flower.

All around her there is the low buzzing hum of beating hummingbird wings as they all try and take their fill.

They chase each other away from the feeder they've claimed as their own. Our hummingbird hasn't got a spot, but she spies a bigger hummingbird distracted by a rival.

This could be her moment . . .

. . . swiftly our little hummingbird hovers closer and closer, until – quick – she dives in.

The hummingbirds are too busy to notice the two children watching them, their faces pressed up against the window. The children watch the sun glinting off their feathers, changing from iridescent red to bright purple to deep shiny black.

Hummingbirds are my favourite bird in the world. I remember the very first time I saw a Rufous Hummingbird, when a kind birdwatcher invited me to his yard (in Lone Pine, California). We watched the birds dancing around the feeders, humming and sparkling.

Our hummingbird is on the move again – she flies and flies and finally arrives at her winter home in Mexico. Look! She's found the patch of red flowers that she feeds from year after year. She greedily gobbles up the nectar after her long journey.

Hummingbirds will find a reliable source of food so they don't have to waste time and energy looking for their next meal. Our hummingbird focuses on refuelling, because migration doesn't stop – she'll need to travel again soon. She will get very feisty if other hummingbirds try to muscle in, chasing her rivals away with a snap of her bill and an angry gleam in her eye.

Other birds aren't as lucky as her, with two places to live, and pit-stops on her journey between them. Because the planet is getting hotter, lots of her friends have lost the places they live and have nowhere to go – and the problem gets worse each year.

This hummingbird is fortunate to have caring humans who give her a helping hand with their birdfeeders.

ARCTIC TERN

Back to our Arctic Tern, who hasn't stopped since we last left her. Criss-crossing the ocean between Europe, the Americas and Africa, she makes her way south.

Our Arctic Tern has been travelling for weeks now, covering tens of thousands of miles over endless waves. There has been no sight of land.

She has reached the tip of Africa and there – in the distance – she spots a group of small islands! She leads the flock of terns she is travelling with towards them. They can briefly rest their wings and fill their bellies full of fish, before they continue on their journey to Antarctica.

They join flocks of terns that have already made it this far, swooping down to meet them on the quay. Some perch on the jetty, others settle on the rocks.

The harbour is full of small fish, and the terns spend the next few hours plunging into the water to catch and eat them. Our Arctic Tern is very full and, after two months of migration, very tired. She tucks her head under her wing to finally have a rest from flying and a proper sleep.

After school, the kids on the island rush to see the thousands of Arctic Terns that have stopped for a rest right by their homes on Tristan Da Cunha – the most remote group of islands in the Atlantic Ocean. Peering through borrowed binoculars, they admire the terns' sharp black caps and bright red bills.

Every year the Arctic Terns fly by on the horizon, and sometimes, like this year, they pay the island a visit for a day or two. This is a sign for the children: spring is on the way! But our Arctic Tern can't stop for too long . . .

BAR-HEADED GOOSE

A Bar-Headed Goose looks much the same as any other goose except, as its name suggests, it has two black bars on its white head.

Over the summer, our geese have been living peacefully in the vast mountains of Mongolia, breeding beside a lake, which stretches across the width of the valley. Here it is sunny for hours each day and there is plenty of fresh grass for the whole gaggle to graze on.

During the summer, the geese barely see any people, there are no roads nor any villages nearby, and only the occasional young yak-herder disturbs them.

Our Bar-Headed Goose hatched out of her egg only this summer and has spent months following her mum and dad around, gobbling up all the food she can. Finally, her real feathers have grown, replacing the fluffy down that covered her before.

And just in time too – the cold winds of winter are already starting to whistle through the high mountains.

Heading off with her flock of friends, our goose knows that she has a very, very long way to go before she can rest again. The migration journey she is about to make is impressive for many reasons, but one of them is because of the humongous distances she will fly. On her first day she flies nearly a thousand miles, heading south over China!

This is all new to her, but she has been built to do this and her strong wings propel her through the air at speed!

Starting to enjoy herself now, she honks to the other geese.

It is her turn to have a go at the front of the V.

From there she spies a group of children waving to the geese as they fly by.

Ahead of her now, the mountains are getting higher, but this isn't a problem. The special thing about the Bar-Headed Goose isn't just how far it can fly, but how high!

She prefers to fly over the Himalayas – home to the tallest mountain in the world, Mount Everest – rather than around them. This is a perilous choice that no other birds would make. But she wants to follow the shortest migration route (who would want to fly further than they have to?) and this, of course, means travelling in a straight line.

To get over these mountains, our goose must fly up to 7,300 metres into the air – so high that even helicopters can't fly here! The higher you go, the thinner the air gets, because there is less air above squeezing it downward. A helicopter wouldn't have enough air to push down on, but somehow our goose manages to carry on flying.

Up here there is also less oxygen, so it is much harder to breathe, and it is really cold. This isn't an issue for our goose, though. She has superpower adaptations: her special blood helps her get more air when she breathes, and extra warm feathers stop her wings from getting too icy as she flies.

Our goose has never done this before and she wasn't sure what to expect. The mountain just keeps getting higher and higher! Looking around, she can see all the other geese look tired too, but the adults carry on, so she knows that she needs to as well.

How much longer can they keep going?

Just when our goose is feeling ready to give up and drop down to the mountainside for a rest, they reach the top of the Himalayas. Snow covers the rock face all around her, and the mountain falls away towards the valleys and fields below. Nepal rolls out in front of the flock, the craggy rocks transforming into green farmland. She is on top of the world!

But there's barely time to rest and the gaggle of geese continue to head south. Even though she is built to fly like this, our Bar-Headed Goose is exhausted by the time she finally arrives at her winter home in India.

The flock spirals down from high in the sky, dropping onto a big wetland lake where they can safely rest on the water and there is grass and roots to nibble on in the surrounding fields. Honking as they descend, they alert the local children, who look up from the game they are playing to marvel at their arrival.

The geese take a winter holiday for the next few months, eating and resting until they'll have to climb high in the sky, form their V, and head back over the mountains again, returning to Mongolia for the summer!

SPOON-BILLED SANDPIPER

Once upon a time, there were hundreds and hundreds of Spoon-Billed Sandpipers setting up their summer home in the Siberian tundra. They arrived just as the snow melted, and would build their nests in the short tussocks of grass beside freshly formed pools.

They spent the summer poking around in the damp moss for spiders and beetles, and snapping flies and mosquitoes from the air to feed their hungry chicks. They watched brown bears wander past on their way to fish in the bay. There were miles and miles of perfect habitat to live in.

Now, there are only two hundred pairs of Spoon-Billed Sandpipers left in the whole world.

This year, our Sandpiper is worried. The Siberian days are already starting to get colder, and this would not be a good place to spend the winter – with its snow and ice, it would be impossible to find enough food.

Yet every year the migration south has become more and more difficult, and she has struggled to find enough places to stop and feed on her 8,000-kilometre journey. Sometimes she finds the familiar places are smaller than they used to be, and she must share them with lots of other birds.

And sometimes she can't find them at all.
But she must get moving, so she sets off . . .

She migrates down the western edge of Asia, travelling along the coast where mudflats and estuaries once ran thick. She's in luck and spots a good place to stop, rest and feed.

Her name, Spoon-Billed Sandpiper, comes from her funny-shaped bill – which looks just like a spoon! This is the perfect tool for this little bird to find her favourite types of food: the shrimps and worms that hide in the thick, dark mud.

She sweeps her bill from left to right, swinging her head from side to side, feeling for food all around her, sifting through the mud to find lots of tasty morsels. If there's food in this mud, she's going to find it!

She is not in any particular hurry, and instead likes to stop at lots of these places and fatten herself up, before continuing her journey along the coast of China.

There aren't as many welcoming places as there used to be, because many nature-rich habitats have been covered in concrete to create roads, ports and blocks of flats.

Our Spoon-Billed Sandpiper (and other migrating waders) needs space to rest, eat and change her worn-out feathers. The good news is that more and more of the remaining places are being protected for Spoonie and her friends.

Our Sandpiper carries on flying, hoping that she will find somewhere to stop soon.

She has left China now and is heading to Myanmar. After miles of coastline, with its big ports and cities and scattered mud flats, it is amazing to head inland. Here she flies over unbroken forest and mighty rivers, but this is not the right home for Spoonie.

Finally, she arrives at a mighty estuary, where two rivers empty their waters into the sea. A secret place, which Spoon-Billed Sandpipers return to each year.

Dropping from the sky, she lands in a huge wetland, hungry and ready to eat.

All the fat she stored to fuel her flight has now been burnt up, and she needs to eat again so she has the energy to complete the last leg of the journey.

The children playing in the rice fields stop to look – smiling and pointing at the little bird with the funny-shaped bill.

Then she's off again . . .

After weeks of flying, our Spoon-Billed Sandpiper touches down on the mudflats in the south of Bangladesh. Finally! This is where she will spend the next few months of her life. Around her, more sandpipers are arriving too, landing in the mud with a quiet splash.

Other waders have come, drawn to the food supply and ready to gorge: greenshanks and plovers and stints land all around her. She only meets a handful of other Spoon-Billed Sandpipers. Lots of old friends are in the group, steadily moving their heads side to side to feed, and also some young birds who she has never met before.

She used to be frightened during the months she spent living on these mudflats, because humans used to come with big nets to catch all the birds living there.

But they don't come any more, and instead she sees them climbing into a shiny new boat, heading out to sea to catch fish to feed their families, leaving the children to play football and cricket on the sandy edge of the mudflats.

Once a month she sees the birdwatchers with their binoculars and telescopes. They come to count how many Spoon-Billed Sandpipers are living here, and she always makes sure her feathers are neatly preened in case they take a photo of her.

I remember taking my shoes and socks off and rolling my trousers up before wading through the gloopy mud in search of the sandpipers, the silt squelching between my toes.

Our Spoon-Billed Sandpiper dips her bill into the mud and starts swaying her head back and forth. Things aren't better yet, but hopefully one day the mudflats will be filled with sandpipers again.

ARCTIC TERN

Now it's time to follow our Arctic Tern again, on the final part of her migration. After more than two months of flying, she tumbles onto the Antarctic tundra. The few birds that have arrived before her squawk a greeting. She's made it! She's exhausted from her 25,000-mile flight.

Feeling the warmth of the Antarctic sun on her back, she knows that her long journey was worth it. Back in the Arctic there will only be a few hours of daylight, and soon it will be dark all day. Here in the Antarctic, she's about to enjoy sunlight all day long. Of all the birds in the world, Arctic Terns spend the most time in daylight as their migration constantly follows the sun.

This will be her winter home. Out to sea, flocks of terns dive for food amongst the porpoising penguins, both looking for a fishy lunch.

Close by on the shingle beaches, massive colonies of penguins spread as far as the eye can see, guarding their newly laid eggs from the scavenging skuas and sheathbills trying to sneak in for an easy meal.

I stand among them, lucky enough to be visiting this magical continent of snow and ice from my home in the UK. I raise my binoculars from the comical penguins and spot the Arctic Terns. I recognize these little birds from the faraway land I've travelled from!

Yes, this is the perfect place for our tern to live for half the year, until the sun starts setting and the cold gets colder. By then, the Arctic Terns will be chasing the sun again, well on their way north on their endless journey around the world.

Take a look around you.

Can you see a bird?

I wonder where they might have been, and what they've seen from their travels through the skies. Our journey has come to an end, but for the birds it carries on.

In a few short weeks they will start their journeys again, this time heading north. Revisiting familiar places, discovering new ones, and then settling down to build their nests, lay their eggs and raise their young.

Continuing their never-ending journeys . . .

For Ayesha, my big sister who made birding cool for me when I was a kid – Mya-Rose

This book is dedicated to my family, friends and agent, Wendi. Thank you for your continuous support – Lynn

PUFFIN BOOKS

UK | USA | Canada | Ireland | Australia | India | New Zealand | South Africa

Puffin Books is part of the Penguin Random House group of companies whose addresses can be found at global.penguinrandomhouse.com.

www.penguin.co.uk www.puffin.co.uk www.ladybird.co.uk

First published 2023

001

Printed in China

The authorized representative in the EEA is Penguin Random House Ireland, Morrison Chambers, 32 Nassau Street, Dublin D02 YH68

A CIP catalogue record for this book is available from the British Library

ISBN: 978-0-241-59792-7

All correspondence to: Puffin Books, Penguin Random House Children's
One Embassy Gardens, 8 Viaduct Gardens, London SW11 7BW